AF428387

EASY READ, EASY LEARN GERMAN LANGUAGE BOOK FOR KIDS

Children's Foreign Language Books

LET'S LEARN
THE GERMAN
LANGUAGE!

German
Alphabet

(ah)

(beh)

(tseh)

(deh)

(eh)

(eff)

(geh)

(hah)

(ih)

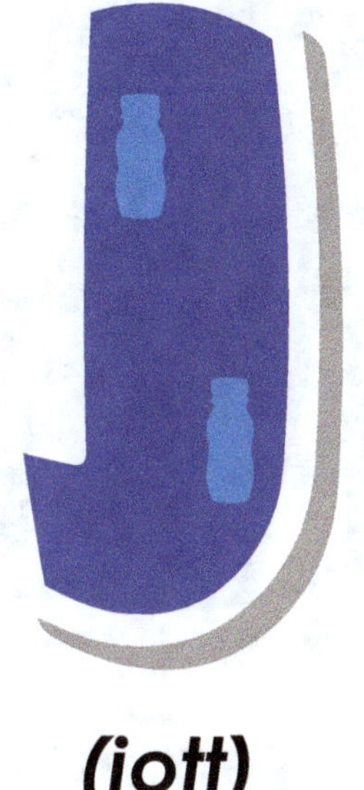

(jott)

(kah)

(ell)

(emm)

(en)

(oh)

(peh)

(kuh)

(err)

(ess)

(teh)

(uh)

(fau)

(weh)

(iks)

(üpsilon)

(tset)

(ess-tset)

(oh-umlaut)

(ah-umlaut)

(uh-umlaut)

Counting in
German

1

eins *(ii-nts)*

2

zwei *(tsvy)*

drei (dry)

vier (feer)

fünf *(foonf)*

sechs *(zecks)*

sieben *(zee-ben)*

acht *(ahkt)*

neun *(noyn)*

zehn *(tsayn)*

Shapes in
German

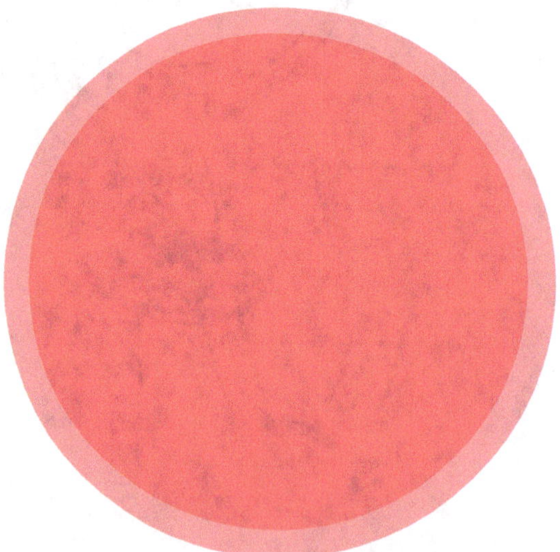

square | das Quadrat

circle | der Kreis

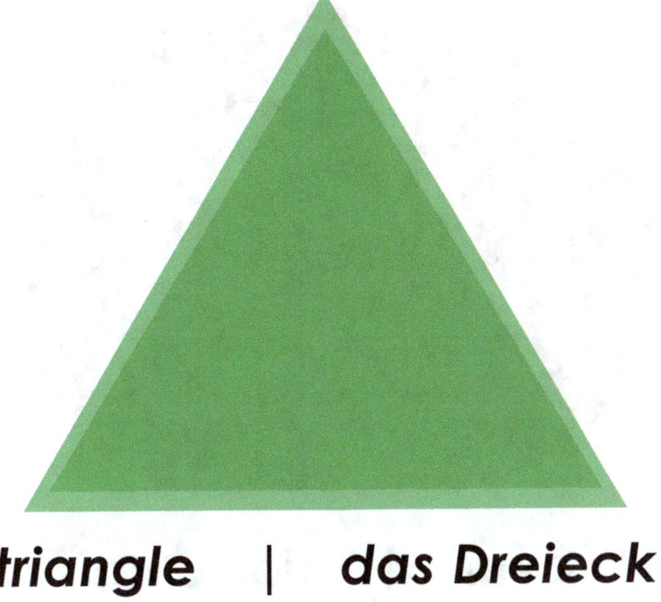

triangle | das Dreieck

rectangle | das Rechteck

oval | **das Oval**

star | **der Stern**

heart | *das Herz*

pentagon | *das Fünfeck*

hexagon | das Sechseck

heptagon | das Heptagon

semicircle | **der Halbkreis**

cross | **das Kreuz**

arrow | der Pfeil

moon | der Mond

Colors in German

red | **rot**

yellow | **gelb**

blue | **blau**

pink | **rosa**

brown | **braun**

green | **grün**

magenta | **magenta**

orange | **orange**

violet | ***violett***

gray | ***grau***

white | ***weiß***

black | ***schwarz***

Family in German

father | **vater**

mother | **mutter**

grandmother | oma

brother | **bruder**

sister | **schwester**

grandfather | **großvater**

SHORT
QUIZ

Write the names of the numbers in German.

4 _ _ _ _ _ _ _ _ _ _ _ _ _ _

6 _ _ _ _ _ _ _ _ _ _ _ _ _ _

3 _ _ _ _ _ _ _ _ _ _ _ _ _ _

9 _ _ _ _ _ _ _ _ _ _ _ _ _ _

1 _ _ _ _ _ _ _ _ _ _ _ _ _ _

8 _ _ _ _ _ _ _ _ _ _ _ _ _ _

Write the German translation of each word.

father _ _ _ _ _ _ _ _ _ _ _ _ _ _

grandmother _ _ _ _ _ _ _ _ _ _ _ _ _ _

sister _ _ _ _ _ _ _ _ _ _ _ _ _ _

mother _ _ _ _ _ _ _ _ _ _ _ _ _ _

brother _ _ _ _ _ _ _ _ _ _ _ _ _ _

Color the image **braun**.

Color the image *blau*.

Color the image **gelb.**

Color the image *grau.*

Color the image *schwarz*.

Color the image *rot*.

Color the image *rosa*.

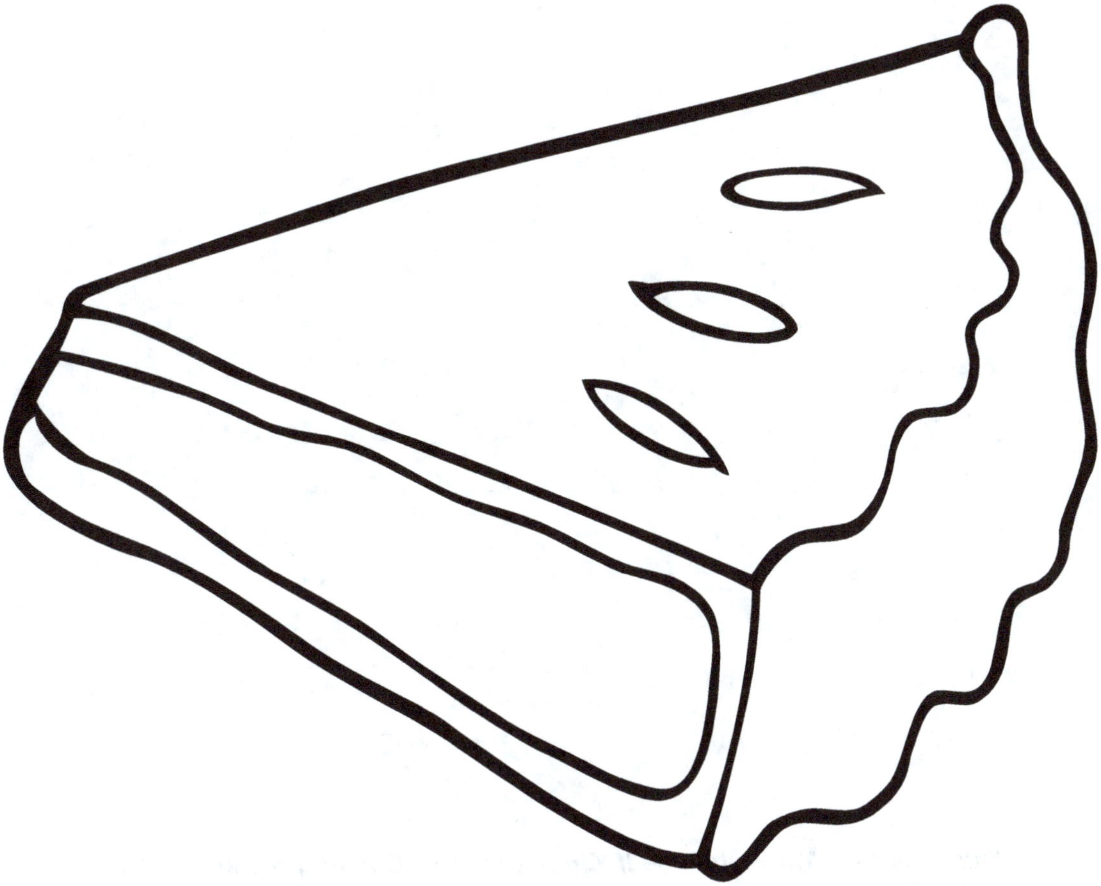

Color the image *grün*.

Color the image *grau*.

Write the german name of the shapes.

- -

- -

Write the german name of the shapes.

- -

- -

Write the german name of the shapes.

_ _

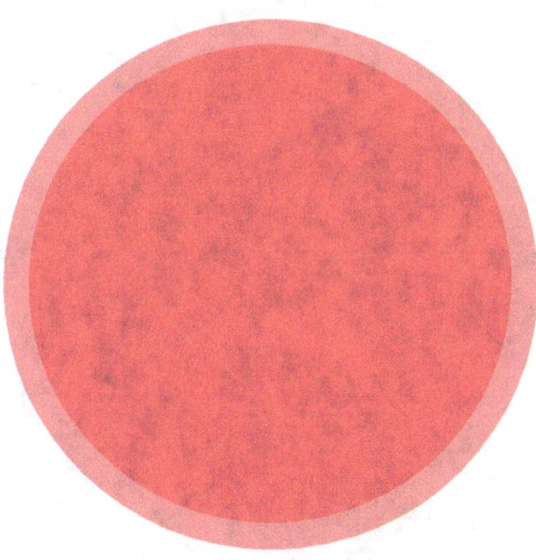

_ _

Write the german name of the shapes.

_ _

_ _ _ _ _ _ _ _ _ _ _ _ _ _ _ _ _ _ _

Write the german name of the shapes.

- -

- -

ANSWERS

Write the names of the numbers in German.

4   vier

6   sechs

3   drei

9   neun

1   eins

8   acht

Write the German translation of each word.

father   vater

grandmother   oma

sister   schwester

mother   mutter

brother   bruder

ANSWERS

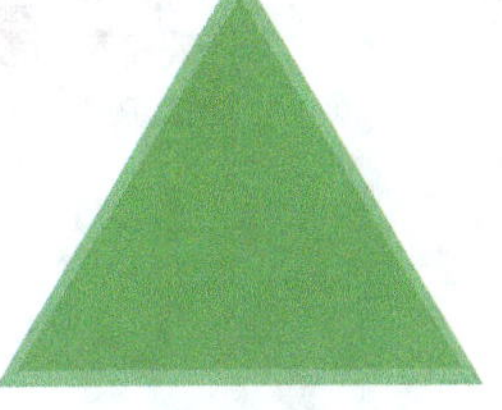

das Dreieck

das Herz

der Halbkreis

der Stern

das Rechteck

das Sechseck

das Quadrat

der Kreis

das Kreuz

das Fünfeck